J577.

£7.99.

WHERE AM I?

This is a snowy place.
It is cold and icy.

WHERE AM I?

By Moira Butterfield
Illustrated by Julia Clay

Belitha Press

JS77

First published in the UK in 1998
by Belitha Press Limited, London House,
Great Eastern Wharf, Parkgate Road, London SW11 4NQ

ISBN 1 85561 794 3

British Library Cataloguing in Publication Data for this book
is available from the British Library.

Printed in Hong Kong

Editor: Honor Head
Designer: Helen James
Illustrator: Julia Clay
Map illustration: Robin Carter / Wildlife Art Agency
Consultant: Steve Pollock

Where am I
in the world?
Read this book
and see if you
can guess.

A lemming lives here.
See if you can find
it in the pictures.

In this place it is very cold all year round.

In spring lots of tiny flowers bloom. Some of them have hairy stems and leaves to help keep them warm.

Many kinds of
insects buzz around
the flowers. Can you
see a bee and two
different butterflies?

Lots of little animals
called lemmings live here.

Lemmings look like
hamsters. They live in
burrows underground.
They come out to eat
plants and grass.

The lemmings must watch out for enemies who want to eat them. Can you spot a hungry fox and a snowy owl with sharp talons?

Some animals only visit in spring and summer.

A herd of reindeer has come here looking for grass to eat. Some baby reindeer have been born. They are called fawns.

Can you spot some wolves following the herd? If a reindeer gets sick and stumbles the wolves will eat it.

Big and fierce animals roam here.

A brown grizzly bear looks for berries and grass to eat. He also catches fish with his long claws.

Bears can walk on all
fours and stand upright.
Can you see a bear on all
fours? It has white fur.

This is the place where polar bears live.

A mother polar bear looks after her two babies. They are called cubs. They will grow up to be strong and fierce like her.

The mother is sniffing the air.
She can smell food from a long
way off. Seals are her
favourite meal.

All kinds of sea birds visit here.

Sea birds build their nests near the sea so they can catch their favourite food. Can you see what they eat?

In summer the sun is always in the sky. That means it is never dark, even in the middle of the night.

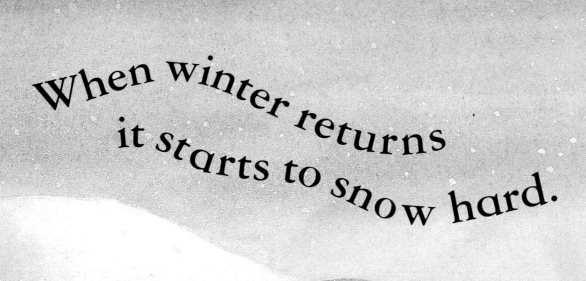

When winter returns
it starts to snow hard.

Soon it will be freezing cold.
Thick snow will cover the
land. The lemmings hide
in their warm burrows
deep beneath the snow.

The reindeer leave and
most of the birds fly away.
They will spend the winter
somewhere warmer.

Only a few animals stay here all through the winter.

The wind howls and the snow is deep. The musk oxen have thick, shaggy coats to keep them warm.

Some animals turn white so they are hard to see against the snow. Can you find a white fox, a hare and a bird called a ptarmigan?

In the middle of this place there is a frozen sea.

The sea animals don't mind the cold. They have a thick layer of fat under their skin to keep them warm.

Can you see a ringed seal eating a fish and two big, fat walruses sitting on a piece of floating ice?

Whales live in the ice-cold ocean.

The whales swim underwater looking for fish to eat. Above them giant pieces of ice float on top of the sea.

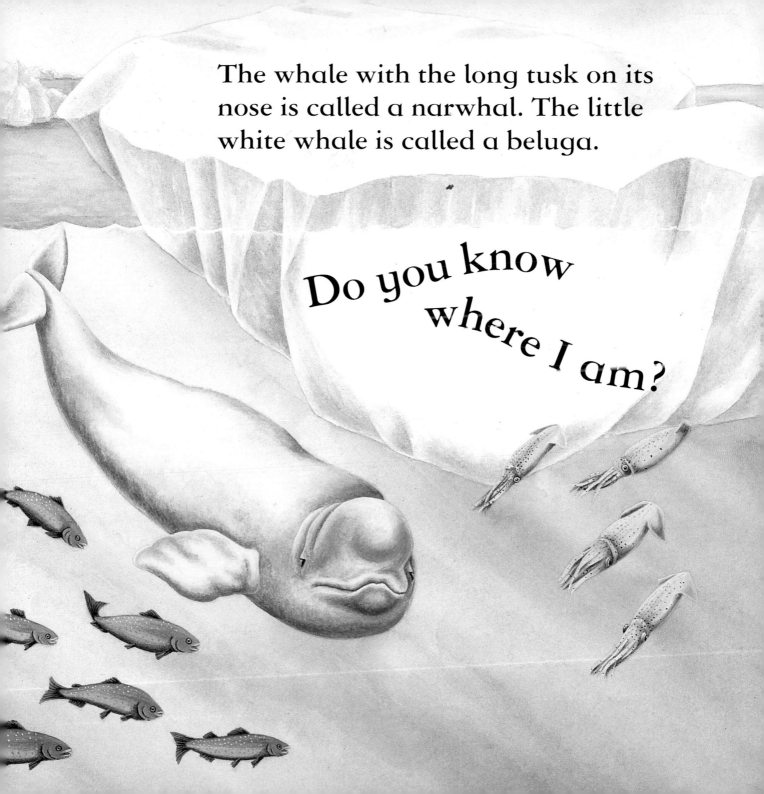

The whale with the long tusk on its nose is called a narwhal. The little white whale is called a beluga.

Do you know where I am?

I am in the Arctic.

Most of the Arctic is a huge, frozen sea
called the Arctic Ocean.

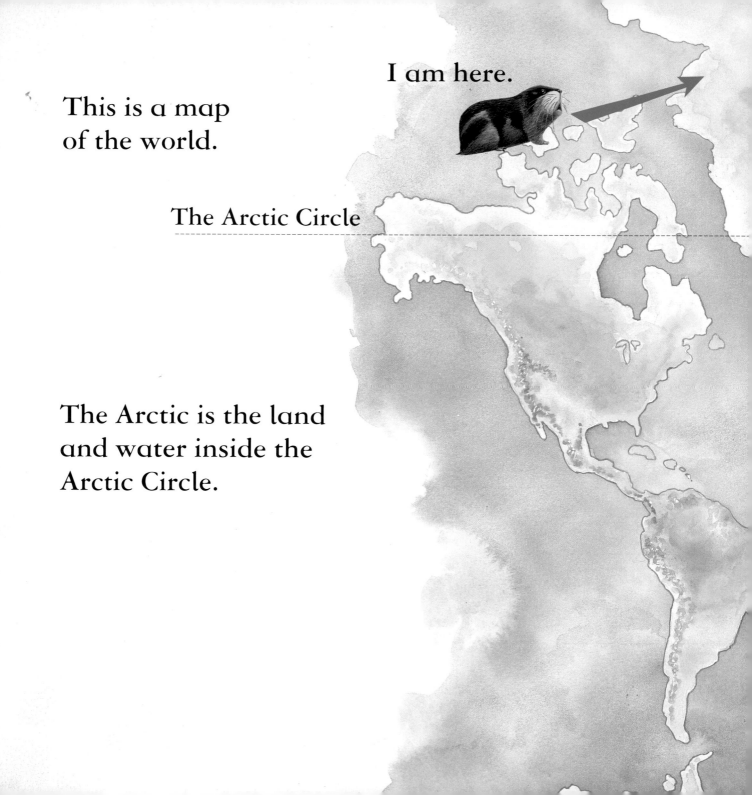

This is a map
of the world.

I am here.

The Arctic Circle

The Arctic is the land
and water inside the
Arctic Circle.

Where are these animals and plants?
Turn back the pages to find them.

Arctic char

Sulphur butterfly

Ptarmigan in summer

Ptarmigan in winter

Little auk

Arctic fox
in winter

Arctic fox
in summer

Purple
saxifrage

Squid

Cranefly

Animal facts

Reindeer grow huge antlers on their heads. A full set takes five years to grow.

Baby seals are called pups. Their mother has to protect them from hungry polar bears.

The Arctic tern eats fish. It dives down and snaps up fish swimming near the surface of the water.

The raven stays in the Arctic during the winter. It is one of the few birds that can stand the cold.

Some groups of geese form a V shape when they fly away to warmer countries.

During one summer a female lemming may have 30 babies. Many of them are eaten by other animals.